VIGNETTES OF
THE WESTERN FRONT

Henry Lawson

VIGNETTES OF
THE WESTERN FRONT

Reflections of an Infantry Subaltern in
France and Belgium, 1917-1918

POSITIF PRESS · OXFORD 1979

Edited by Andrew Lawson

Typeset in Monotype Plantin by Northampton Trade Typesetters, film originated by Adrian Lack at the Senecio Press, Charlbury, printed by Parchment (Oxford) Ltd., and bound by Henry Brooks (Bookbinders) Ltd., in the City of Oxford.

Positif Press, 130 Southfield Road, Oxford OX4 1PA

ISBN 0 906894 00 X

I dedicate these words to my fallen comrades

Contents

6

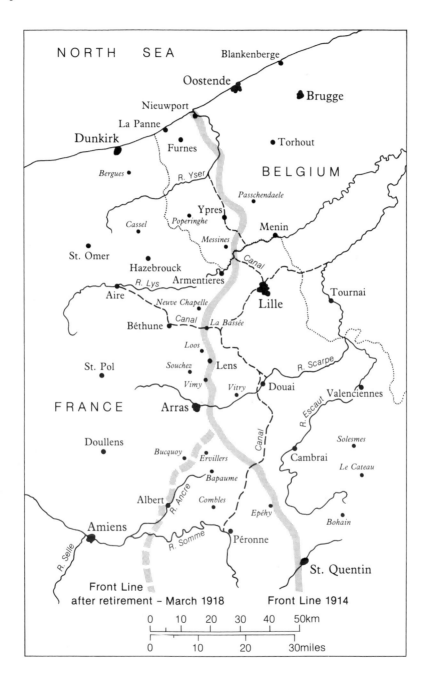

NORTH SEA

Blankenberge

Oostende

Brugge

Nieuwport

La Panne

Dunkirk

Furnes

Torhout

Bergues

R. Yser

BELGIUM

Passchendaele

Ypres

Poperinghe

Menin

Cassel

Messines

St. Omer

Canal

Hazebrouck

Armentieres

R. Lys

Aire

Neuve Chapelle

Lille

Tournai

Béthune

Canal

La Bassée

Loos

Souchez

Lens

R. Scarpe

Vimy

Vitry

Douai

Valenciennes

FRANCE

Arras

R. Escaut

Doullens

Bucquoy

Ervillers

Cambrai

Solesmes

Bapaume

Le Cateau

Albert

R. Ancre

Combles

Canal

Epéhy

Amiens

Bohain

R. Selle

R. Somme

Péronne

St. Quentin

Front Line
after retirement – March 1918

Front Line 1914

0   10   20   30   40   50km

0   10   20   30miles

Foreword

Every war has its historians. Their works are essential to the study of history and they often make fascinating reading; but the raw material, out of which they fashion their histories, is provided by the men who fought and died in the wars they describe. No history, official or otherwise, evokes such a vivid and immediate picture of what those wars were actually like, as do the recorded memories of men who took part in them. Every war produces a few such men. Caesar's Gallic Wars used to be known to every English schoolboy; Raymond of Aguilers and Fulcher of Chartres gave a more vivid picture of the First Crusade than any official record could supply, as did John of Joinville of St. Louis' campaign in Egypt, and Geoffrey of Villehardouin of the capture of Constantinople by the Fourth Crusaders; and those who have read Rifleman Harris' description of the battles of the Peninsular War in Wellington's day will have a far better idea of what that war was like than could be obtained in any official War Office record.

The Great War of 1914–1918 produced men on both sides who recorded what it was actually like to fight in the mud and the blood of the trenches. Henry Lawson was a young officer, who managed to survive the carnage of those days. Towards the end of his long life, he described some incidents which stuck in his memory. They are as poignant and as immediate as flash-light photographs, which have captured for ever moments now long buried in the past. It would surprise me if this little book did not become a classic of its kind.

With a generosity which was typical of him, just before he died he bequeathed the copyright of this book to the Cathedral of Guildford which he had served so well and loved so long. We are deeply in his debt.

Antony Bridge
Dean of Guildford

EPISODE ONE

The Ypres

Salient

Prelude to Passchendaele

A boy of nineteen years of age, I entered the Ypres Salient for the first time on 8th October 1917 to take part in the attack on Passchendaele Ridge, moving out from the battered town of Ypres through the Menin Gate. Before me in blinding rain lay, for thirty or more square miles, a quagmire, an endless chain of shell-holes, filled with slimy water. Tracks of duckboards weaved for miles across the sludge. It was a scene of unbelievable desolation, outrunning sight in every direction, and relieved only by a few battered tanks and odd stumps of trees, the remains of blasted and flooded spinneys. The shells had ploughed every yard of earth. There was a pervading stench of decay over a field of battle that was already more long-lasting and more terrible in its dread and complete destruction than any perhaps in previous military history.

The battalion spent the day so-called "resting" on the Frezenberg Ridge several miles from the front line. We attempted to dig a trench, or even a few holes, as some protection from the elements, but this proved impossible because whenever a spade was inserted one or more decayed bodies were uncovered. So we waited all day in misery for the hour of movement, which was 10 o'clock at night.

The rain was as heavy as ever when we moved off as a battalion along a duckboard track to reach the point of attack, which we had never seen. We were to deploy as best we could before 5 o'clock in the morning of 9th October. This was an unhappy prelude to battle – a sleepless night spent hour by hour moving up the duckboard track starting and stopping again and again in pouring rain, carrying full equipment. However I do not believe that our strength was as sapped as much as might have been expected. There was nowhere to sit down during the prolonged pauses in our progress. Those long hours of approach to a destination marked out only with white tape amongst the water-filled shell holes, was a period of gnawing anxiety and uncertainty. I had heard of the Ypres Salient and the savagery of the contest there, but Passchendaele was only a name, not yet a byword.

The Attack on Passchendaele Ridge

Movement was so difficult and slow that after seven hours we were late and found ourselves caught by the enemy's defensive barrage. We started the attack from a hillock called Abraham Heights, going downhill for about a hundred yards until we found ourselves at the beginning of what had been a wood. There were a few treeless stumps and almost a lake of water. It was impossible to go forward and we were stuck in this morass with the Germans firing salvo after salvo of 5·9" shells at us. At the height of their intensity the shells fell so closely together that six would come down every few minutes within about an acre.

Although I had already spent some seven months in the front line in other sectors I had never before experienced a bombardment of that severity, nor indeed did I afterwards in any of the great battles that were to come. If the ground had been dry my company would have been obliterated. As it was, the shells penetrated so deep into the mud before bursting that only men very close to the pitch were killed or wounded. Even then in the first two hours of that hell on earth there were enormous casualties. In my company we had lost half our men before breakfast. We had made no progress whatever. I myself was hit some half dozen times by spent pieces of shell, luckily without a wound.

The company commander had been wounded and left me in charge. We were directed to retire a short distance up the hill behind us to find somewhere to dig ourselves in and seek a little cover. There we stayed for three days and three nights almost incessantly under bombardment from the German guns. I was in a small shell hole. The conditions were unutterably apalling – the rain, the wet and the dead bodies all around. I remember vividly a German officer, stretched on his back perhaps twenty yards from my hole, no helmet, tall, very fair hair, not a mark on him, the most beautiful figure of a man I have almost ever seen. Periodically I used to go and visit him and dwell upon this pitiful waste of manhood.

The Wounded and the Dead

I walked around the company as often as I could. Whenever men were hit they invariably sent for me, because they wanted to shake hands before either they died or went wounded to the dressing station. Their eyes were eloquent. By looking into them, as one tried to bring comfort or to ease pain, one could be almost

certain whether the goodbye was final or not. Although they might not be able to speak or find words there was sometimes a quality in their gaze suggesting that they were giving thanks for past favours and friendship and expressing regret that the end of our comradeship had come, the future totally unknown. I remember especially a splendid corporal of mine with whom I had developed a special rapport in the course of long months working together. He was in a shell hole, propped up by his fellows, his head terribly crushed by a heavy piece of shrapnel. The instant I was summoned, I assumed the worst. When I joined him I knew that my assumption was correct. He could hardly speak, but he took both my hands in his, looking into my eyes and talking to me with his eyes, while awaiting the arrival of a stretcher. He was still clinging to me when carried away. In retrospect I can only think of David's superb lament over the death of Saul and Jonathan. Paraphrasing the Bible account, it might be said that in one of the fiercest battles in modern history he had been slain in a high place and that one of the mighty had fallen. He was lovely and pleasant in his life.

The Survivors

There we remained, as I have said, for three days and for three nights, almost incessantly under bombardment. When the time came for us to be relieved by Australian troops, I was spent and horror stricken; shaken by the unending experience of apprehension and bloodshed. The survivors, including myself, dragged our feet back to the Menin Gate down the path of duckboards which I was to come to know so well throughout the coming winter months. I recollect seeing sickening hallucinations on the walls near the Gate as I passed through, images of the carnage, friend and foe dead or dying, stretched in the mud under a leaden weeping sky.

The Fire and the Rose

Abraham Heights, the site of our endeavour and endurance, is adjacent to the place chosen for Tyne Cot military cemetery, the largest Commonwealth cemetery in Europe. After the war, when

I visited the cemetery it was clothed in roses, shedding an aura of peace and tranquillity. Some of my men are buried there in known graves. The names of others, whose bodies were unidentifiable or never found are inscribed upon the memorial at Tyne Cot or upon the walls of the Menin Gate, now reconstructed. The battle for the Passchendaele Ridge began on 31st July 1917 and ended early in November. The advance on a seven mile front, penetrating between three and five miles, cost some three hundred thousand dead, wounded or missing. That, however, is not the full story of the series of desperate engagements in the Ypres Salient from 1914 until the end of the war. It has been calculated that over the four years the casualties exceeded half a million men of whom ninety thousand of the dead were either unidentifiable or have no known grave. The names of these ninety thousand are carved in stone on the Menin Gate or on the memorial at Tyne Cot, gathered under the words:

"Here are recorded the names of officers and men of the armies of The British Empire, who fell in the Ypres Salient, but to whom the fortune of war denied the known and honoured burial given to their comrades in death."

The headstones of the unidentified are marked with the words "Known unto God". The Menin Gate holds by far the greater number of names and stands as a symbol of the sacrifice of all who passed that way and did not return. Every evening still all traffic is stopped and the Last Post is sounded from the Gate, a fact not widely known perhaps except by the survivors (now small in number) of those battles fought so savagely in the worst conditions.

T. S. Eliot in his poem Little Gidding, which concerns the dead in a churchyard, says "the communication of the dead is tongued with fire beyond the language of the living". Is it possible for anyone gazing in awe at that seemingly endless list of names not to absorb much in addition to the names? These dead men speak in silence to us and to future generations with tongues of fire pleading the cause of peace and the realms of spiritual life. The whole poem insists that one day humanity will find that "the fire and the rose are one" when "all manner of things shall be well".

In 1925 Sir Philip Gibbs wrote:

"Not a thousand books will ever tell that story in its full detail of heroism, sacrifice, adventure and individual experience."

and again:

"But to all men, who walked through that City and the roads beyond, where they were in the flaming heart of war, this ground will ever be haunted by that noble youth of ours, by those muddy men in steel helmets, by the surge of transport and guns, by the ghosts of a great army of youth, so cheery even on the edge of abominable ordeal, so valiant in the face of death itself, so patient in suffering, so stubborn in endurance, so simple and splendid by the faith that was in them and never told. 'They were a wall unto us both by day and by night' up there in the Ypres Salient, which is sacred ground because of their sacrifice."

Military historians will argue indefinitely about the Passchendaele battle. I am now aware of the strategy, namely to break through quickly during the summer and to force the enemy from the Channel ports, which harboured their shipping and submarines. But the tactical question is whether the attack should have been pressed when the advance had begun to take much longer than expected and when the climate and ground conditions had deteriorated. The use of tanks was impossible and the movement of guns difficult. Further, the small German forts of concrete (nicknamed "pill boxes") dotted all over the place and housing their machine guns, were impervious even to a direct hit from a light shell. They made a major contribution to the huge casualty list. The resistance to our progress had, I think, been underestimated. I still wonder whether the High Command before ordering a continuance of the advance to the final objective had first inspected closely the field of battle and had assessed the magnitude of demand upon stamina and perseverance. Had the many factors and circumstances been weighed in the balance? As a loyal subaltern upon whose youthful shoulders some small part of the burden of complying with the orders fell I must assume that the answer to that question is in the affirmative.

The Occupation of Passchendaele, Winter 1917–18

The Ridge was taken in November 1917 by Commonwealth troops with unmatched gallantry in conditions as bad or even worse than ours had been. Subsequently we occupied the outlying posts over the top of the Ridge for three months. The journeys up and back again were dangerous because the German heavy guns were pin-pointed on sectors of each track of duckboards. But again, while the wet weather continued, one could stand on the track amidst the falling shells, splashed of course with mud and water, but virtually without risk as the men, in groups of ten or so hurried past in single file.

Burying the Dead

On the first occasion we reached the top after dark (moving by daylight would have been suicide) and found the abandoned German dead lying where they had fallen. Their identity disks had to be removed and their bodies buried. Before throwing the bodies into the mud, dug quite shallowly, I used to try to read some of the words from Chapter fifteen of the First Epistle of St. Paul to the Corinthians, then generally recognised as the funeral lesson. Of course no torches could be used and I had to try to follow the tiny print of my pocket Bible by the light of the guns' flashes and the flares that were being sent up from both sides. But largely in vain, for in a matter of minutes the shells of the German field guns began to pass us on the crest, too low overhead for comfort. For the burial I turn to the graphic words of Reverend Studdert Kennedy from "The Rough Rhymes":

> *"And that night I'd been in trenches*
> *Seeking out the sodden dead*
> *And just dropping them in shell holes*
> *With a service swiftly said"*

Those lines of Studdert Kennedy possibly refer to the first battle of the Somme in July 1916. But for me they represent the epitome of the tragedy, death, and suffering of the Salient fought over again and again during the four years 1914 to 1918.

He then goes on to portray the scene even more graphically:

"We stood up to give the blessing
And commend him to the Lord
When a sudden light shot soaring
Silver swift and like a sword.

At a stroke it slew the darkness
Flashed its glory on the mud
And I saw the sergeant staring
At a crimson clot of blood."

Exactly my experience too. I had so often seen the Verey lights soaring and illuminating "No Man's Land". In place of the Blessing, which was not mine to give, I asked the men to repeat after me the Lord's Prayer.

Thus we went on our way, still in drenching rain, to our posts in nearby shell holes.

No Orders to Withdraw

Our second visit to Passchendaele Ridge was on a windswept night with heavy rain. Apart from the usual dodging of heavy shells on the track coming in – perhaps six miles in length – we settled without incident into holes in the ground, which were already six inches deep in water. Our position was a hundred yards beyond and below the crest of the Ridge, the enemy being many hundreds of yards away. The storm increased and by midnight our holes were a foot deep in water and still rising. At about one o'clock I struggled back to company headquarters and asked permission to retire to the crest of the hill where the ground was drier. I said that if the men had to stay where they were, I could not guarantee to bring anyone out in the morning alive. My request was bluntly refused and I had to return. However, my instinct was correct: in fact an order had been given to withdraw outposts, but the order did not reach my company.

The sequel occurred at dawn when the usual barrage from our own field guns was laid straight along the line of outposts supposed to have been withdrawn. My impression at the time was that our eighteen pounders were like pop guns compared to their German counterparts. One shell fell no more than a yard from my head in my flooded hole merely scattering a little mud without even shaking me – a quite unimportant detail, but somehow retained in my memory. Doubtless the ineffectiveness of the barrage was attributable to the sodden ground. Nevertheless a close call. Although we suffered no casualties I was thankful when the ten minutes ordeal was finished.

On another visit, when the ground was frozen hard, the story was different. Life did indeed become really dangerous as heavy shells, bursting upon impact with the iron hard crust, hurled splinters a considerable distance in every direction. Before making any movement we had to guess whether the guns were likely to open up again. The Salient was less evil in appearance, but still deadly if one was unfortunate. Nevertheless casualties were few.

Reflection

Going back on leave one night from Passchendaele Ridge I took the duckboard track alone in the full moon, sauntering sometimes

La Bassée

Earlier, in March 1917, the first sector of the line I had helped to occupy was known as the La Bassée front. It was a quiet area lying on both sides of the famous canal. The northern side was a mining area and on the south were the brick stacks. Each brigade of the division held its proportion of the front line continuously for almost four months without relief in reserve. The baptism of fire was not alarming as one soon accustomed oneself to shell fire and sniping. One learnt immediately that any shell one could hear coming would almost certainly prove harmless and the same applied to the swish of bullets. There was danger only from shells that burst before one heard them, and from bullets which passed so close to one's head that they cracked. Far worse was the "Mini" so called by us, which was a mortar carrying a heavy explosive charge, invariably causing casualties, most of them fatal, if it landed in a trench. I shall never forget the stench of cordite after such an episode and there were a number of them. We also experienced a concentrated dose of phosgene gas. The few who failed to adjust their gas masks in time endured perhaps the acme of suffering until mercifully claimed by death. One still shrinks from the ordeal of such bestial weaponry. Mustard gas was different and I shall have something to recount about that later.

Undermining

For a time my platoon was sent to occupy the most distasteful point in the front line. This consisted of an underground "sap" leading up to a firing post for six men, sticking well out into the mine craters in "no man's land". Apart from the sentries, we sat for four days on the floor of the tunnel, and we could hear, immediately under our feet, the sound of "Tip, tap. Tip, tap. Tap". The Germans were driving a tunnel underneath our tunnel, with the intention of exploding a mine under our trenches. For us it was a situation of continual anxiety. Each day our engineers came up to make an inspection with their instruments. They said that the mine was not ready to go off, but that they would call again. One could hardly fail to observe the hurry of their departure. And as I was going to be there for four days and four nights I always said to them, very ostentatiously, "Thank you. And goodbye". I never heard the ultimate outcome.

The Patrol

This sap was nearly my undoing when I led out a patrol one night. I thought that for a change we could pass along our line about midway across "no man's land" and call upon another advanced post in our line. I gave appropriate notice of the time, route, and purpose and we set off at midnight. What happened has for ever remained inexplicable to me. We crawled along the rims of craters and at about the right time reached wire in front of an obviously manned post. I was leading and I stood straight up and called "halloo" to be answered by a shot from the rifle of the sentry a few yards away. By the light of the rifle flash I recognised a German helmet and instantly realised that by some ghastly mistake I had almost entered the enemy's line. How the sentry missed me at such close range and how we all escaped, crawling, while the rifle fire increased under a canopy of lights rocketing up over us, I shall never understand. The Germans sent out a patrol when we were half way home, but miraculously they passed quite close without seeing us.

Thus a foolish and ill-judged little jaunt ended safely without loss. My nerves were in tatters. The predicament was entirely my own fault. A lesson not easily forgotten. One should not have "played games" for the sake of variety, even between friendly outposts of our own line when the territory was equally controlled by the enemy.

An Easter Breakfast

On Easter Day 1917, I was in the line at the brick stacks by the La Bassée Canal. The dawn was glorious and the day remained peerless, so appropriately for the Festival. No Church Service was held for us, but I was determined to have my egg for breakfast, which had been hoarded from a farmyard behind the lines. I planned another breakfast treat to mark the day, and alone, immediately after dawn, I slipped down to the Canal and cast into the turgid water half a dozen Mills grenades. The explosions killed many small fish, which floated to the surface. I collected them and they were fried by my batman together with the egg. I felt almost civilised and enjoyed the meal, never giving a thought to the contents of the canal where the fish had been living.

I cannot recollect a single shot being fired by either side throughout the day. I am sure that the meaning of Easter, its holiness and joy had been in the minds of friend and foe alike. I thought that with a little ingenuity Holy Communion might have been provided for us front-liners in so quiet a sector. But that was not to be.

False Alarm

We spent one charming weekend at the brick stacks on the south side of the La Bassée canal. It was dry and warm, and without incident save for one extraordinary episode that caused near-hysteria among the men of my platoon holding the front line. At dusk and throughout the night there came a loud and sinister croaking sound, echoing across no man's land from the low ground behind German lines. Within minutes of the overture of this orchestra I was hurriedly summoned and told that the Germans must be preparing a new secret weapon. I think that the ranks and N.C.O.'s were more truly frightened then than at any other time in the war. But my interest in natural history was to stand me in good stead. Having lived since childhood on Surrey Commons I was familiar with the nocturnal sounds of the country-side. This was even a pleasant and delightful memory of my young days on summer evenings. Therefore I laughed and said that the noise was only the homely evening calls of bull frogs which gather in ponds and marshes in early spring in amorous congregations. No matter how I expostulated not a soul would believe me. I even quoted the frogs chorus of Aristophanes "BREKEKEKEK KOAX KOAX" to be met with blank scepticism.

I talked long trying to pacify fears, which were ludicrous to me, although to the men's suspicious minds, uneducated in nature, this was a threat most terrifying in its unknown and unimaginable portent. I recognised for the first time that not one of them knew anything about country sounds or about the natural history of bogs and ponds. It emphasised for me the gulf between the life of the town-dweller and the life that I had been given in the country with its privileges and opportunities.

I should probably have shown more sympathy because, I think, no-one slept a wink that night. I could hardly have expected them to have heard of Aristophanes and the chorus of frogs in his play. But my innocent and simple explanation was beyond their comprehension and wholly unacceptable. Under conditions of life and death, with the Germans no more than a minute of running time away, assurances are difficult to convey. Their fear was perfectly genuine. I made a special effort by searching for a bull frog croaking on our side of the line. My luck was out. More I could not do to allay the trepidation lasting for many hours.

A Distant Battle

There was a dramatic dawn on June 7th, 1917, when away some fifteen miles to the north, the British launched the battle for the Ridges of Messines. I was sitting as usual alone in our front line in utter stillness. By a strange trick of sound, I did not hear any of the colossal explosions when the mines laid under the Ridges were blown. But I could hear the tremendous drum fire of the guns and in the dark I could clearly see the flashes of the immense assembly of artillery ranged to support the infantry in assault. We had been for months in static service, holding the line in a quiet sector to gain experience and to accustom ourselves to trench warfare. So I had not seen a great attack before, even at long distance. To say the very least, I was impressed and I watched with eyes glued to the scene until the rising sun and morning light gradually outshone and finally blotted out the spectacle. I marvelled at the power displayed and eagerly awaited news of the event and its outcome of complete success. It never entered my head that later on I should, myself, be leading in several vaster offensives under similar barrages.

Homesickness

After the novelty of trench life had turned to a monotonous routine, a feeling of homesickness occasionally welled up within me particularly during the night watches. On the one hand there was a certain pride in standing and holding the very frontier of our country's fortunes; on the other a longing to return, even temporarily, to a normal civilian life. Strangely, it was the homely whistles of the steam trains, heard far away on the clear night air, that brought to me the feelings of being caught up and strangled by obligation and sense of duty. In the front line there were no other sounds from the far flung villages and towns. As I walked up and down or sat awhile, listening to the shadowless silence that enclosed me (there were many more dead silences than non-combatants would assume) I gazed at the stars, as Milton said, through the empty vaulted night. I mused across the gulf that separated my labours from the world of my family at home. A silence, touching time, and being of itself as deep as eternity, can be more moving than the tearing roar of battle.

Holiday by the Sea

On the extreme left of the British line during July and August 1917 we were stationed near La Panne on the coast where, in a sense, we enjoyed a seaside summer holiday. Evidently the High Command had destined us for a great attack on the Nieuport sector, but the Germans forestalled them and the strategy was abandoned after we had occupied the line for a short time.

The holiday was only spoilt by the enormous congregation of jelly fish in the sea, so that bathing, which we did regularly as a battalion, was painful in the extreme. We were stung all over and there appeared to be no antidote. The beach was level, the sea quite shallow. We all waded in and as soon as we had washed,

we hurriedly departed, leaving the jelly fish to their own territory.

Of course we had no bathing trunks, and the battalion completely naked was a sight to see. Certainly the Germans thought so. Perhaps for fun they occasionally sent round a small craft with a machine gun, which ranged along the surface of the water from maybe half a mile away. As the shells skidded off the water or passed just overhead I never felt so naked in my life. The whole battalion got out of the sea quicker than one might have believed possible and fled into the dunes at the back, naked and covered in sand. I do not remember any casualties. Once, I believe, we succeeded in retaliating along one of their bathing beaches. These adventures were not very serious, a kind of horseplay rather than warfare.

The Sacrifice

I record only one haunting incident – if the death of an individual in war is no more than an incident. The canal and the river Yser separated our lines from the Germans' and we were expected to send swimmers across at night for information. Volunteers were called for and one of my corporals was selected. Blacked from head to foot and with a lifeline around him, he was quietly launched in total darkness. After a time the line broke somehow or slipped and he was swept away. Those who heard his cries for help, which we were powerless to provide, will never erase from memory the rending pathos of his absolutely helpless loneliness and certain death as the succession of his echoing calls fell more and more faintly and distantly. Finally his cries ceased, reminiscent of Tennyson's "And answer echoes answer, dying, dying, dying". The loss of this splendid figure from the company left in our hearts the silence of desolation, a depth of grief more shattering even than the death of a man in battle by one's side.

I would defy anyone living with death, as I was for so long, not to be moved by pity and compassion in the trauma of such momentous events, however humble the part played by the individual himself. Consider one aspect only, the series of letters which I had to write after each battle to the parents of the men I had lost. What might one say? It seemed to me that there was no tangible reward for their sacrifice. No particular glory, no presentation of a decoration, only a name to be carved on a war memorial. Their true heroism, which might have been honoured had they survived, was stripped from them with all else of materiality. I feel that there was a parallel, in a sense, in the coronation service of our Queen when she came to her anointing in a simple white garment, all her jewellery and orders having first been removed. Those men, stark in their death, came to their anointing by the sacrifice of life, their souls hallowed, their memory and achievement left to us in benediction and gratitude.

EPISODE THREE

Everyday Life

in the Trenches

Living Conditions

Historians do not usually describe what routine life was like under the conditions of war. At the beginning of my service all the front line trenches held two feet of water and thigh-length waders were essential. Only the fire steps were above water. Splashing my way around my platoon once with my heavy equipment, I became stuck in the mud and required the assistance of two sappers to extricate me.

Dug-outs, even in the front line, afforded some comfort from the elements although they were a very flimsy protection against the enemy's guns. I preferred not to sit in one when we were under bombardment. Later when we took over the German constructions we found them in every way superior to ours, stronger and deeper. At times there were no dug-outs for rest and shelter. On one front line tour I sat for four days and for four nights on my steel helmet in a scooped-out hole somewhere on the side of a trench. Doubtless an irregularity but the only method of obtaining rest.

In the dug-outs we warmed ourselves by charcoal fires that gave off obnoxious fumes. There were sometimes beds with wire mattresses and tables for eating and writing. Hot food was fetched or brought up daily, mostly bully beef, for which there were forty recipes, or a mixture of meat and vegetables, extremely good, called *maconochie*. Of course we had fresh meat and vegetables when available.

We each had an adequate bread ration and in addition there were army biscuits four inches square and one inch thick, which my then sturdy young teeth were unable to penetrate. Tea was of course the staple drink. On the whole we fared pretty well.

In the line each man carried a water bottle, but drinking from it was strictly forbidden except under orders. Sometimes the front line was cut off from supplies and at such times the contents of the water bottles had to be stretched out to last several days.

I was never ill, and did not even catch a cold, which would have been a frequent occurrence at home. The same applied to almost everyone. I suppose that our good health could be ascribed to an outdoor existence, similar to that of primitive man; tough, but spent in the elements, day and night, wet and cold, hot and dry.

Rats swarmed through the trenches. Sometimes I tried to shoot a few of them until I concluded that the foray was more dangerous to my men than to the vermin.

Grime and Lice

I cannot remember having had a hot bath in a bathroom throughout my service overseas. However I did have a portable canvas bath to hold a small quantity of hot water that was boiled by landladies and attended to by my batman. In a completely static sector of the line, when we had held the trenches for eight days we were entitled to use facilities in the rear where the men could have shower baths. Sometimes the officers used these too.

The problem of keeping oneself clean was greatest when we were in movement, for example during the great German offensive of 1918. Then there was no opportunity of removing a vestige of clothing for at least three weeks or a month, let alone having a thorough wash. In any event water was in short supply. Lice, little grey parasitic insects, were everywhere and clothing had to be fumigated at regular intervals. An ingenious doctor attached to the battalion once devised a sort of sauna bath inside a very small ramshackle bivouac covered with blankets. One sat on a bench in the pitch dark and steam from a boiler induced intense perspiration while one washed with a huge cake of soap. The sensation and cleansing were delightful and I went back again and again as the days passed before our return to the trenches. That was a time when the lice had really got a hold in our clothes and gave us continual irritation.

Routine

There was always work to be done during the day on the trenches, repairing revetments or improving the parapet. There was heavy work to be done if a shell or a mortar bomb had exploded in the trench. At night the wire protecting our front was repaired when necessary and a patrol, often conducted by myself, sent out into "no man's land". There was an understanding that the first half of the night belonged to us for that purpose, whereas the second half was relinquished to the enemy. It was certain to lead to an engagement, if the convention was broken.

The regular night patrols into "no man's land" were primarily regarded as maintaining an offensive spirit, rather than as a source of information of importance. An early task each day was to write up the report of the patrol sent out the night before. This had to be in substance absolutely truthful but there was always the problem of writing anything beyond the bare facts of timing, distance and route of the patrol. I would not deny that there was occasionally a temptation to embroider a little colourful detail.

The Clandestine Report

There happened to be one officer in my company entirely different in character and accomplishment from all the rest of us. He was very popular and rather a friend of mine. He was an aesthete with the appropriate appreciation of fine things, literature amongst them. In civilian life afterwards he obtained great distinction, his appointments and honours filling half a column in *Who's Who*.

One evening my friend was ordered to conduct the normal patrol in "no man's land". I did not see his written report because he did not consult me. But the next day he received a tough rebuke from the colonel who called his report abysmal or words to that effect. He was deeply grieved at the criticism. Knowing him much better than the colonel did, I shared his disappointment. His qualities had always impressed me and I felt that injustice had been done. I proposed therefore to put matters right to the best of my ability. I asked whether I might do a patrol for him the next night on two conditions, first that he would sign my report as coming from himself and second that in return he would write for me a doggerel rhyme about our company. This was a gift he possessed to a brilliant degree.

We sealed the bargain and I set out towards midnight. I took extreme care and was out in "no man's land" for an hour or more. Luckily the night was dark and the line quiet. I crawled with the patrol for about a hundred yards along the enemy's wire, noting its strength and weaknesses, locating in the process three enemy posts. We were near enough to hear them talking, but unfortunately none of us understood German. Nevertheless, I had got the material I wanted, certainly enough for my clandestine report.

The report was prepared, signed and sent in. The result was electric. Next morning the company received a memorandum from the colonel congratulating the officer signing the report, which he proposed to circulate as a model, so comprehensive and succinct were the contents. My friend was delighted and I was amused. I had no idea that one day I should spend my time drafting legal documents. He had his ballad ready and I more or less entered into a standing arrangement to repeat the exchange with him. Alas he did not stay much longer with us having found a far more responsible appointment elsewhere. I know that I was wrong because I had taken more risks of death or capture than I would normally have done. Youthful indignation might be offered as an excuse, but not as a justification.

Officer's Watch

There was always one officer of the company on duty, each officer usually taking four hour watches and making the rounds with his batman. I invariably chose the night hours up to morning "stand to" at dawn, when the rum ration was distributed. I carried a rifle in preference to a revolver. The trenches were zigzagged and our posts about twenty yards apart. One could never be certain in the dark that no marauding German had crept in between the posts. Caution was the keynote and a weapon handy. The enemy lines were only an average eighty yards from our own.

My second choice was the next watch from dawn to break-fast. My reason ? To be in solitude in the glow of the early morning sun when I could watch the wildlife in "no man's land". I saw and heard larks, partridges, pied and yellow wagtails, occasionally quail and once a pair of kestrels hopelessly confused by the anti-aircraft shells bursting around them. Those were hours of happiness as though the whole realm of nature was mine. Closing my eyes I might entrance myself into the belief that I was still at home in Surrey fields on a golden May morning.

Letters Home

Although trench routine was dull at quiet times we were always in touch with the outside world because the postal service was excellent. I wrote to my mother almost every day except when movements and action made it impossible. Most of the men of my

platoon wrote home to their families and girlfriends regularly. One of my duties was to censor the men's letters, sometimes quite a labour when they were illiterate. There was little of real interest that I felt justified in reporting in my own letters; censorship was very strict.

Similarly our in-coming post was excellent, though letters accumulated when we were constantly on the move, as we were in the last months of the war. Most weeks I received several letters from relations or friends. My mother worked her fingers to the bone in knitting socks and mittens for the men. This care was deeply appreciated as were the regular food parcels of cakes and other eatables.

There was no trouble in ordering from London shops. For instance if I wanted a new pair of breeches I merely wrote to my tailor and was promptly served. Likewise one communicated with one's bankers, a straightforward and often pleasant task, because there was so little to spend money on, and our accumulating bank balances cheered us up. The one purchase I expected to need, but never did, was a spare pair of pince-nez glasses, which I always wore on account of my short-sight. In fact I never broke a pair and cannot remember the pince-nez even falling off my nose, notwithstanding all the clambering, crawling adventures recalled in these vignettes.

A Short-Sighted Examination

My moderate short sight almost prevented me from getting a commission for active service. On leaving school I had tried for Sandhurst, but was turned down because of my eyesight. Then on the advice of my father I made another attempt through the Cambridge University Officers' Training Corps, followed by the Officers' Cadet Training Unit (OCTU) based there. When the day of the medical examination came I was in trepidation. We were put in an ante-room where we stripped naked before passing into the doctor's room. Warned by my previous experience I took everything off except my pince-nez and on entering the medical chamber looked immediately for the board of letters used for eye-testing. I saw it at once propped up in a corner and, while being examined, I memorised the letters. The daunting moment arrived when the doctor said "take your glasses off". Would they put the board up showing the side which I had memorised, or would it be turned round to reveal that there was another lettered side? To my relief the board was held straight up. I had to be careful not to overdo my preparation, thereby risking detection. It would have been an elementary task for an optician to fault me by checking my glasses. So I started fluently and gradually slowed down until the doctor said "that is enough". I could have jumped for joy. Thus great personal concerns turn on trifles. I have often wondered how many good men were lost to the fighting forces through the meticulous observation of the medical standards of the day.

Leave of Absence

Leave was fairly generous though it depended on the state of affairs on the Western Front. During my twenty months in France and Belgium I had three periods of leave of a week each, at home or visiting relations. The travel facilities were excellent and on my return journey my father always came with me to Victoria Station to see me off. The farewell was much more emotional for him than for me, for I was anxious to rejoin my platoon before any important engagement.

Once and once only I left the line to make a social call on a neighbouring division where my younger brother was serving in a pioneer battalion behind the line. How I got to know of his whereabouts may have involved a breach of security regulations, but our adjutant, when I requested a day off to visit my brother, treated the request as a perfectly normal diversion and sent me off with his blessing. The journey and search occupied the morning and I at last appeared to the astonished gaze of my brother who had no idea from where I had materialised. We spent a pleasant afternoon together discussing family news and comparing the lives we were then living.

The Chaplains

Personally I had little to do with the doctor because I was never ill. Similarly I did not see the chaplain frequently because he did not come into the front line, doubtless very properly as he was a non-combatant. There was one exception to this, a chaplain of our battalion who was intensely interested in what went on up at the front. We were discussing this one day when I said that if he really wanted to share our experience of front line duty, I would take him with me on a night patrol into "no man's land". My conduct was almost certainly irregular, but fortunately all passed without a hitch. Afterwards I believe he looked upon us with a fresh insight. One did hear of tremendous deeds of bravery by chaplains, some of whom were awarded high decorations. Much was due to them all. Their proper place in the action was at the first field dressing station, where casualties were brought in, the sight sometimes horrible beyond words. As I was always in the front line I never had any idea of what went on at those dressing stations, at least until I was wounded and then I was unconscious most of the time. Nevertheless, I can imagine what the doctors and chaplains had to do, probably under shell fire, with limited resources, their duties unending, and no glamour of victory to exhilarate them. That was a task of self-giving on a grand scale.

Social Life

Looking back and making a reconnaissance as it were, of our relations with others in the battalion, I am astounded how circumscribed our existence was and how closely we kept to ourselves in our company. When we were resting there were small dinner parties. We invited the officers of another company and vice versa, the menu consisting of what was at hand. We might have been fortunate enough to get a lift in a truck to a neighbouring town where shops were open and life normal. But during action in the trenches, we had little contact with other companies as we all had our separate sectors to hold.

Outside the battalion I knew no one, neither machine gunners, sappers nor other specialists, certainly not even those manning the field guns giving protection to our lines. In many ways that was a pity, but we infantry subalterns had little time to spare for social visits. Out of the line in the autumn, while we were recouping our strength, I used to watch the gunners hunting partridges. The countryside was bare and open and they pursued the coveys of birds on horseback. Partridges cannot fly far without coming to ground and so it was possible to exhaust them and knock them down with sticks. I used to envy the savoury game dinners prepared for their messes.

Within the company, though, there was plenty of time for talk. Reading matter was scarce. The men of my company were all from the Oldham district of Lancashire. They delighted in telling me, in effect a foreigner from the south, the stories of their lives, particularly the gay times spent on holidays. As in W. J. Cory's poem *Heraclitus*, "we tired the sun with talking and sent him down the sky". We sometimes used to lie out under the stars, and an almost invariable subject for conversation was the fabulous delights of Blackpool in wakes week. They gave me a vision of

magic casements, stately pleasure domes and enchanted towers. I listened in amazement as they talked of driving up and down the esplanade, spending with gay abandon every penny of which they were possessed, other than the half crown left under the clock on the mantelpiece at home for payment of the cab on their return. In civilian life they had been cotton spinners and factory workers and in those dark days they warmed their hearts at the remembered flame of their Lancashire homes.

Many of the men gave me photographs which still hang in my home. After the war there remained a close fellowship between us. When all was over I corresponded regularly with the survivors, and still do so with the sole survivor still living. After I married I invited them to stay at my home and there we talked of the old days almost with nostalgia.

EPISODE FOUR

The German

Offensive

Defensive Reinforcements

My division was in reserve at the critical moment when the Germans launched their offensive on March 21st, 1918. We were rushed to the battlefront in hundreds of London buses. The weather was perfect, sharp frost at night, sunshine all day; everything was to the advantage of the Germans, even the early morning mist giving them some cover and helping them to penetrate our lines.

From the buses we were bivouaced in a wood north of Bapaume, where we were far too cold to sleep. I walked up and down all night. At dawn we were on the march, advancing to meet the enemy, who had entirely overrun the existing defensive front. For me action started on 24th March at a village named Ervillers, which we found had not yet been occupied by the enemy. I sat in the sunshine all morning just outside the village, my platoon being part of a reserve, listening to the endless rattle of the Lewis gun and rifle fire of the troops defending the village. The sound was similar to that of Bisley Ranges near my home in Surrey multiplied tenfold with some intervals of only spasmodic rifle fire as the Germans were stopped and forced back. There were no artillery or cavalry on either side; only infantry with rifles, machine guns, and Lewis guns facing one another.

The advance of the Germans had been on a fifty mile front penetrating to a great depth. Obviously the situation was extremely serious. Only a week before, I had been on leave at a theatre in London, which was normal in appearance, full of troops and civilians. Now as I sat behind the front line in the sunshine my mind inevitably turned back to those few days earlier. I thought of the enormous difference to our strength if only a part of that leisured mass had been available with rifles in their hands. I wondered how anyone could enjoy or even attend a theatre if they were aware of the terrible threat.

A Commander's Quandary

About two o'clock in the afternoon I was sent with my platoon into the line facing the advancing Germans. There I found an assortment of men from miscellaneous regiments, disorganised but doing their best despite fatigue beyond measure. They had been driven back from the original defensive lines and were in a small trench, probably first occupied by friend or foe in the late stages of the Somme offensive in 1916, which had been followed by the retirement of the Germans to the Hindenburg Line.

My distinguished Company Commander has only recently revealed to me the sequence of events that led to my platoon being sent into the line in the teeth of the German attack. The Colonel had ordered him to send a platoon to plug a gap which had developed on the left of the line. This order placed my Company Commander in a quandary. Which platoon was he to send? The situation was so desperate that he believed the selected platoon could only face death or capture. He felt sure that he would not see them again. He has told me that he wanted above all to keep my platoon, and that he had so resolved. Upon reflection, however, he changed his mind, considering that no matter how great his personal regret he must do his best for the battalion. Thereupon he sent me.

Of course I knew nothing of these deliberations at the time, and ultimately all was well. But to me now this is a fascinating instance of a basic truth. Dire decisions concerning the lives and fortunes of one's men have to be made in war on the spur of the moment and they often depend merely on a whim of choice. Matters of great magnitude can hang on tiny considerations. The more senior the command, the greater must be the ordeal of decision, perhaps overcome finally only by a total rejection of attachments and by an absolute absorption in the current demands of circumstance.

The German Advance

In the open undamaged country before me were the advancing Germans. A description, which I wrote at the time, described the German tactics as follows:

"The Boche came on in ones and twos and small groups, apparently disorganised and yet with wonderful speed and method. In a few moments hundreds would filter down into a depression of the ground, and from there advance in small sections, running anyhow, one after another, making an exceedingly difficult target. It was not easy to inflict heavy losses with a rifle, though at times we had good practice on odd parties. The pace at which they came on and how they managed to pile up line after line of men in successive attacks was almost incredible. One minute you would be watching the crest of a ridge seeing a few men sauntering over the top in twos and threes, and two minutes later you would find the face of the ridge swarming with men and more and more pushing on behind. As fast as their lines were shot down, other lines took their place."

As I watched the scene it was clear that they vastly out-numbered us. Several times two airmen of the Royal Flying Corps with much bravery flew down in their small biplanes to about twenty feet above the ground, well in front of our line, and blasted away with their machine guns probably causing con-siderable losses to the enemy. I admired their intrepid enterprise.

Altogether during those afternoon hours we were very much "eyes front". That being so, I never noticed that my platoon was becoming more and more isolated. Others alongside us had been creeping away and vanishing, under orders to retreat. At about 6.30 p.m. I suddenly realised that my platoon was alone, faced by a multitude who might at any moment stroll over and take us. I had had no orders to withdraw and I suppose that was one of my really lonely moments in the whole war. We were left to our fate, to perish or to surrender. As I mused, my Company Com-mander taking a considerable risk suddenly rushed down and said "withdraw at once". I never obeyed an order more promptly or more gratefully. We withdrew to a wood in the rear, where we set up outposts and there was a roar of triumph as the enemy entered Ervillers and found the village empty. This shouting was an example we never followed when, shortly before the end of the war, the position was reversed and we were taking village after village. Maybe it was a custom of the Germans, although I never heard it again, presumably because we were soon to stand to the last with further retreat not even contemplated.

The Retreat

We started to retreat again during the night. In the morning, marching along a road to what proved to be our final standing line we were caught by some shrapnel from the German guns that were following us. I had not seen the effect of shrapnel in the open before and I was appalled. The buds of the trees lining the road were just opening and their branches were cut to ribbons. A section of men about fifty yards ahead of me were swathed as with a scythe. We scattered and the treatment mercifully was not prolonged.

About midday I was shown into an old shallow trench north of Ablainzeville, with a fine view over the country far ahead. Immediately in front of us the ground sloped down to a dip, into which we could not see – dead ground. In the dip were huts. Our field of fire, then, was barely forty yards. On our right was a small wood.

The Guards Officer

None of us had had any food or water for some thirty six hours; the horse drawn transport could not function on the blocked roads to the rear. We had water bottles full of water but no permission had been given to take a drink from them. Having put the men to the task of deepening the trench and making it defensible I looked over to the troops holding another trench two hundred yards away with an unmanned gap between us. I decided to walk over to introduce myself, partly as a friendly call and partly to discuss the frailty of our very thinly-held line and the gap between us. I found they were the Guards Division and an officer was watching my arrival. He was immaculate as if he had just stood down from duty at the Palace, although his experience during the last forty eight hours must have been as traumatic as

our own. I shall never forget the horror with which he looked at me. My lips were swollen and nearly black because I had not had anything to eat or drink. Talking with my dried-up tongue was painful. I had three days' growth of beard on me. I was absolutely filthy from top to toe. He looked me up and down as he would a mongrel and enquired what I wanted. I replied to the effect that as his neighbour in a perilous situation I thought that he might be interested to know who was holding the line next to him beyond the gap. He was perfectly polite, but exuded and projected an overwhelming air of infinite and effortless superiority regarding past, present and future. All he said to me was:

"Good afternoon. Nice of you to come over. We don't need anything, thank you. Goodbye."

I crept away astounded. I believe that his division was relieved that night which accounts in part for his indifference to my plight. My admiration for the Guards has been and remains unlimited but I did inevitably reflect upon their physique and fitness in comparison with a territorial infantry division like my own.

There is a Second World War counterpart to my experience of the Guards. Prof. R. V. Jones in his book "Most Secret War" writes of the return of the troops from Dunkirk. He and other witnesses were amazed at the discipline and bearing of the Guards arriving at Victoria Station and the contrast between them and the remnants of other regiments.

Backs to the Wall

All the while the German army was deploying and moving slowly towards us without hurrying, but with deadly precision. I had a seat in the front row of the stalls. The sight was amazing. I could make out their infantry with officers on horseback, Red Cross wagons, guns, the commissariate, the lot. They were so ordered, they might have been on manoeuvres. They were virtually out of range although occasionally I tried a really long shot to let them know that we should mean business when they reached us. By dusk they had come to the huts in the dead ground, perhaps a blind mashie shot away if one were an old fashioned golfer. There they stayed, to my astonishment, for the whole of the fortnight that we stuck it out in our inadequate trench, first in the dry cold, later in rain and mud. The presumable explanation came along after; we just happened to be at the hinge of the vast salient they had carved, which was not to be widened.

Little happened during the first night of our sojourn in our tiny trench. But the morning at dawn was quite another matter. Not unexpectedly, German snipers under cover of darkness had occupied the little wood on our right so that they could enfilade our trench. Our every movement brought shots, the only solution being to lie down except for the look-outs. Fortunately the company facing the wood judged the situation to a nicety. After they had sprayed the wood liberally with Lewis gun fire the ardour of the snipers was dampened. Peace reigned once more and work on strengthening our trench continued.

We had absolutely no protection, no wire and no field guns. At that moment I received, on a pink field telegraph form, Field Marshal Sir Douglas Haig's famous declaration of "Backs to the wall". After reading the words I looked behind. I could observe no support of any kind except perhaps one company of our battalion. I judged rightly or wrongly that the land as far back as the Channel Ports was void of any "wall" and that we were on our own. I took the message around the platoon suggesting that when the frontal attack came, as I was sure it must, each one of us should try in the seconds available to take two of the enemy with us before we were shot down. I was fairly handy with a rifle and after measuring the ground in my mind's eye I thought I might even manage three. That was a decision of elementary acumen. Courage played no part, merely discipline to decree of the Commander-in-Chief. Our resolution, often openly spoken of, weighed heavily upon us for the attack might come at any hour of the day or night. I am sure that the apprehension and the suspended uncertainty between death and life which was held over us for so long and never out of mind, stretched tension occasionally almost to breaking point. The period was nearly fourteen days and nights, although after four days a few field guns returned to cover our front and a little wire was brought up. There was no mention of relief, and we knew that our position would be hopeless if we were attacked in strength by the enemy who were still comfortably ensconced in the dip below us.

A Moment of Panic

Once my nerves must have got the better of me. I decided to call
on the intelligence officer at Battalion Headquarters, although I
had no need to do so. It was just a whim on the spur of the
moment. I found him at the bottom of an old dugout which had
no steps leading down into it. There was only a long, steep muddy
slope of perhaps twenty feet. I slid down and after our talk I
tried to scramble out. But I slipped and slipped until claustrophobia caused me to panic and scream for help, which would have
been entirely unnecessary had I quietly manoeuvred myself up
the slope. But by that visit my life was actually saved, because on
reaching the front line I found there, in the very middle of the
hole under the parapet where I had been sitting all morning, an
unexploded eighteen pound shell, fired from one of our own
field guns. Death would have been instantaneous if I had remained there. Yet again my escape had been miraculous, unless I
was protected by the caring hands of Providence.

Bayonets and Gas

Day after day passed and we became more venturesome. One
mid-morning a corporal of mine set off with three men to patrol
along my side of the little wood. I had a perfect view. They
came to a fallen tree and suddenly a hidden German leapt out
when the patrol was only a yard or so away. The corporal, an
athletic man, sprang in a flash and drove the bayonet on the end
of his rifle straight into the German; it was a reflex action, un-
believably swift, but in complete accordance with our frequent
bayonet practice on hanging stuffed sacks. Earlier we had seen in
the Ypres Salient an Australian soldier and a German locked in a
macabre embrace of death with bayonets through each other.
But never before had I seen the grim deed performed – a hand to
hand encounter of the most fearful aspect. I imagine that the
German had neither seen nor heard the patrol coming.

Later, we moved back from the front row of the stalls to the
first row of the balcony. Here the trenches were deep. Hearing a
quiet "plop" sound, repeated over and over again I proceeded to
investigate. As I did so, a gas shell pitched right into the trench

not more than a few steps in front of me. We were being deluged with mustard gas. In the few seconds before I could adjust my gas mask I breathed in a whole mouthful of the stuff. I felt a sharp burning all down my throat and in my lungs; not necessarily fatal as with phosgene gas, but enough to make me murmur to myself "so this is it". I lay down on my back on a shelf in the trench to do all I could to expel the swallowed dose. To my

delight, after five minutes the burning sensation eased and in fifteen minutes I was up and about again with the men. We presumed that the gas was the prelude to an attack. The Company Commander and myself were the only two officers who were not casualties. Together we set about organising the defence while the shells were still dropping. We removed the gas masks from our faces, but were careful to continue breathing only through the

mouthpiece. Wherever a gas shell had exploded, the soil around was contaminated and would burn flesh even through clothing. I cannot recall a death from mustard gas. It was very injurious, nevertheless, though not the torture of the damned, inflicted by other gases.

Easter Day, which had meant so much to me since my childhood, fell in this period, during wet and mud. No Church service was possible because we were still holding the line in a vital area. That must have been the most disagreeable Eastertide I ever spent.

New Hopes

After the great German offensive was spent, checked, then pushed back a distance, our division was allotted a quiet sector of the new line. In view of the enemy's enormous losses another offensive on our front was not expected, but one could never have dreamed that within three months the allies would begin attacking without cessation and that the war would be over by November. At the time, even as low down in the hierarchy as my small and insignificant platoon a new, optimistic outlook was becoming felt, having been imparted by Marshal Foch to all beneath his sole overall command in what had been in effect a beleaguered garrison. The secret I know not. The change was inward, partly due, no doubt, to the first arrival of the Americans in France. A stimulus and a refreshment of spirit and a feeling of long drawn out hope began to run through us all, as at last we were starting to see a unified strategy as had never been unfolded before.

An Initiation

My first contact with the American army was a visit paid by an infantry officer, about the rank of colonel, to me in the front line trench as usual on a glorious May or June evening at 7 o'clock. The trenches were dry, deep, and in good order. I was sitting on a fire step contemplating how good life was when the American officer, with his escort, arrived. He said to me:

"Is this the war, Mr. Lawson?"

"Yes", I said, "it is indeed the war."

He said, "It's very quiet isn't it?"

I said, "Well it has its quiet moments, but sometimes it has its rough times too".

"It's quite extraordinary to me" he said. "But where are the Germans?"

"They're about sixty to eighty yards across there."

"But I hear nothing going on."

I pointed out that neither side wasted ammunition. He showed disbelief whereupon I asked one of my men for a spade. I threw a few grains of soil over the parapet of the trench to attract the attention of the sniper opposite. Then I held up the spade, blade uppermost, above the parapet. Within seconds there was a crack and a hole neatly drilled in the spade, which I held out to the Colonel. After glancing at the spade and looking searchingly at me he never uttered another word. I have always felt that he was like the rich man in the Bible who walked sorrowfully away. Afterwards I wondered what his inmost thoughts really were. I hoped that I had not been unkind, but the lesson, if it were a lesson, must have remained with him for the rest of his days.

A Harbinger of Peace

Often we lived in a wood when resting; a lovely little place full of spring and summer scents and sweetness. I was interested in butterflies and moths. Once I found on a stem of grass the most perfect specimen I had ever seen of *Hylophile bicolorana*, a gloriously vivid green moth with white underwings, having just emerged from its chrysalis and dried its wings. At the time I was talking with our Company Commander lying in the shade of the trees. I drew his attention to this miracle of nature's beauty and speculated whether it could be a harbinger of peace. I derived comfort, a kind of companionship, from this cycle of natural life within range of the shell fire and the total destructiveness of war. I have frequently sensed that all mystery finally lies in the order of creation, its development, and regeneration. I was fortunate to have been brought up with a sufficient outline knowledge, though elementary, of living creatures to obtain solace and immense pleasure at so tiny a discovery. Such moments were priceless for the recruitment of spirit in preparation for the next round of fighting. The unexpected discovery of this perfect moth, which I have never forgotten, did indeed prove a precursor of the peace we all longed for, but alas only after the heavy losses, many amongst our own company in the great offensive battles that were to lead to victory in a few months time.

The Sniper's Skill

Another episode of those summer days was my initiation to the sniper's skill. A miniature range about thirty five yards long had been built in a hollow. I enjoyed practising there with a ·303 rifle, there being no miniature rifles. An officer, a particular friend of mine, had just attended a sniper's course that had included the use of telescopic sights. We others only had the use of open sights. He asked me to shoot with him one evening and he began by shooting fairly accurately his initials with bullet holes on an ordinary miniature range target. Then, having removed his autographed target he set upright on the metal frame a spent ·303 cartridge case. To my astonishment he performed the seemingly miraculous feat of making the bullet stick in the cartridge case exactly half way through, forming an elegant cross. Probably a commonplace little effort nowadays amongst the military, but entirely novel to me.

American Involvement

An American infantry contingent was attached to us for training, to learn something of our battle experience. I had hardly anything to do with the training although I often talked with them, advising them not to underestimate the Germans, in particular their deadly machine guns. They were all raring to have a go, as keen as mustard, and most of my words fell upon deaf ears. They were unable to comprehend a defensive war that was static for long periods, presumably because their freshness of mind, body and spirit outshone our dour persistence that had become ingrained after years of trench warfare. They brought a refreshing new outlook to the front. The heroic and reckless deeds of courage of the American infantry in the last months of the war must always be remembered with gratitude and boundless admiration. Their list of casualties speaks for itself. If a bell ever tolled for gallantry it should have tolled for their lost thousands upon thousands.

The Baseball Match

Turning my attention to amusing them I proposed to our Colonel that we should have a baseball match. He agreed, saying that we must make something of the social occasion and that he would invite the Divisional General. With the Americans I marked out a pitch on the German side of the wood never anticipating what was to occur. It was a fine evening and we were all assembled, the Divisional General mounted on his magnificent black charger, the two teams, and onlookers. When I went in to bat (if that is the right term) I found the first two balls unplayable, dipping and turning as they shot past me into the keeper's hands. Then I heard a heavy shell coming and, as though I were playing in a test match at Lords when someone moves behind the bowler's arm, I withdrew and sat down. The approach of the shell being audible I knew that it would not pitch amongst us. In fact the explosion was quite sixty yards away. I waited to see whether another shell was coming and then stood up to receive my third ball from the pitcher. I looked around. There was not a soul in sight except some of our people sitting on the ground laughing. The General's charger had jumped three feet into the air and was now disappearing at full gallop across open country; afterwards I was told that it had covered three miles before it could be pulled up. A discussion followed when our opponents and others emerged from the wood. Obviously common sense had to prevail and the game was abandoned. Apparently an enemy balloon had spotted our game; the question was whether the sending of the shell was semi-humour or whether it was a ranging shot and one of many. Although the game was thwarted, the evening was a general success.

War in the Air

In the line the principal change was the appearance on both sides of balloons, fixed to cables and manned by observers. The air force on each side tried to shoot down in flames their opponents' balloons. Sometimes they were successful and the occupants floated down to the ground on parachutes. The respective air forces, while patrolling the lines, fought innumerable battles in their biplanes. I cannot to this day imagine how our pilots, without any protection, braced themselves to the trepidation of shooting it out. Machine gun fire was fearsome enough down on ground level, but in the air with a void underneath, supreme

dedication and the highest courage was surely demanded. I saw many planes shot down in flames, never without a catch of breath and a horror-struck shiver for the condemned pilot. Once I came across the imprint of a man's body, arms outstretched, legs straight, every detail marked six inches deep in dry ground. The impact must have been colossal. In a way these intrepid fliers were relatively defenseless, compared with us infantry. The

same applied perhaps to the artillery, who had to submit to savage counter-shelling where they stood. We infantry were better off to the extent that we had some range of movement and when we were in the offensive we felt the thrill of participation at the very heart of the fight. With one exception we infantry men seldom suffered the same privation as the artillery. The exception was when parties from other battalions carried out raids to identify the enemy or to take a few prisoners from the enemy front line, using our front line as a starting and returning base. The enemy would retaliate by throwing up a defensive barrage, which would reach us in the front line, stuck in our trench and shelters where movement or evasive action was impossible. One felt frustration and claustrophobia such as the artillery must have felt when hammered by an enemy barrage, immobile under fire.

An Act of Mercy

One dawn, seeing a German patrol still out in "no-man's land" we managed to shoot one of them before they reached the safety of their trench. Immediately another man jumped out on top to recover the body of his dead or wounded colleague; a brave action indeed. At once I ordered my men to stop shooting and to leave the German free to his act of mercy. Whether I did right or wrong I cannot judge, but pity overruled my role of killer. However, to mark the respite and to underline the moral considerations, we subsequently sent a burst of fire over the precise point in the trench where we had permitted the rescue to be made. Whether the example would have been followed in a reverse situation I doubt, and maybe I should have quenched my moral scruples.

Saved from Suicide

As a mere platoon commander, naturally and rightly I had no idea when, or even if at all, we should join in the great offensive begun in July. I was dining one night with the Colonel when he mentioned that the Brigadier disliked the enemy salient of a few trenches exactly opposite my normal position in the line. Possibly he was weighing the prospect of an offensive at the appropriate moment. Rashly I told the Colonel that I would undertake to eliminate the salient and straighten our line on condition that enough strength for the effort would be provided. I had seen too many raiding parties cut to pieces for little gain. The Brigadier must have been intrigued, because he sent for me. I asked for two tanks, which were not available. Instead he said that we would use gas.

The preparations were made, a date fixed, and the gas prepared for an attack soon after dawn. I had not thought much about the danger, but I asked the chaplain whether we might have a communion service on the evening before, just behind our location in the reserve trenches. All such services were to me impressive with piled drums covered with a white cloth, acting as an altar, but this particular service has stood out in my mind through the years whenever I have taken communion.

As we all partook I remembered vividly my Confirmation, when I first absorbed those beautiful and comforting words "He was known to them in the breaking of bread". Having made our peace, accepting the risk of death only a few hours later, we put the finishing touches to our preparations. Then quite unexpectedly the direction of the wind changed, making the use of gas impossible. The plan was cancelled and only then did I begin to understand more clearly what I had been about. The officers of the battalion had considered that I was being suicidal in the part of the attack I had allotted to myself and a few picked men. We were to advance on the salient from a flank, exposing ourselves for a distance to the machine guns from the main enemy line. Thus I was saved from my reckless folly. Looking back now I think that I perceive a sense of destiny in the many hazards and escapes encountered up to that point and later throughout the vast offensive battles that followed.

Interludes

behind the Lines

Discomfort Preferred

There were rest intervals when the division was out of the line. Someone, particularly if he had been in the Second World War, might wonder whether we really were at rest, unharassed by shell-fire or bombs from aeroplanes. In my case, with two exceptions, the answer would be "Yes". We lived quietly in the countryside in the early days of my service, officers often in a farm house, the men in barns, training and turning out for parades. There were even French beds in the houses, muffled bundles of feathers, although I preferred to sleep on the tiled or wooden floor so accustomed had I become to sleeping hard. The landladies were very good to us, never appearing to worry about a possible German break-through, although the enemy lines were sometimes not many miles away as the crow flies. The sole disturbance was when we were within reach of the line at La Bassée and the cottage assigned to me was surrounded by a battery of guns. After a time even their fire did not awaken me lying happily on the floor the great bed beside me unoccupied.

The first of the two exceptions was, I think, at Poperinghe behind the Ypres Salient when we were living in huts. There during the winter of 1917–18 the odd aeroplane or two came over after dark to drop a few small bombs. One could see the aircraft caught in the searchlight beams with anti-aircraft shells bursting near them. I never saw one of these aircraft brought down, but once a bomb hit a hut very close to mine and there were casualties. No cover was provided against such raids, neither slit trenches nor shelters. Probably the labour was considered unnecessary in view of the sparse damage a single aeroplane with small bombs could do occasionally. That must sound strange to modern ears, but in my time even late in the war the aeroplane was not looked upon by the infantry as presenting a danger. Flying was still in its infancy.

Naval Bombardment

The other exception was at Hazebrouck rather further away from the line than Poperinghe. There we had the novel experience of being shelled by fifteen inch naval guns. I was billeted in a comfortable house with a nice dining room. We sat down to lunch one day when suddenly we heard a whistle blown, then the thud of a distant gun firing, followed long afterwards by a mighty explosion in the neighbourhood. Naturally we made enquiries and learnt that at intervals Hazebrouck was subjected to such bombardments presumably because it must have been an important centre of communications. Certainly my battalion had no casualties and the days passed with a recurrence of the three-fold drama at intervals of a whistle blown, the thud of the gun's firing, followed some time later by the explosion. We were amused rather than worried. Again I cannot remember anyone thinking of taking cover, even if any had been available. Maybe we were fortunate. The idea of the enemy using fifteen inch naval guns against us infantry would have been a strange fantasy. Railroads, stores and ammunition dumps must have been the target.

Target Practice

There was an unexpected incident when my platoon was performing an exercise under the inspection of a General. There had been a divisional platoon contest, which my platoon had either won or had obtained a place in the final before the competition was abandoned for lack of time.

That may have been the reason why we were put into the particular exercise that became our undoing. We were given live ammunition and we had to manoeuvre up a grassy hillside for about one thousand yards, targets being placed on the face of the hill. There was a small group of cattle grazing between the starting point and the targets to which I paid no attention. All seemed to go reasonably well. On arrival at our destination the General began to make some observations and comments of approval until suddenly he stopped and said 'What is the matter with that cow?" I looked round and sure enough there was a cow collapsing and falling to the ground. The General then exclaimed "And there is another one!" I could only hang my head in shame.

Others may have been in the exercise, but there could be no doubt that my platoon was responsible. We had to pay heavy compensation to the farmer. I have no recollection whether we had the beef! Naturally I was ashamed at the cruelty to the animals. My own investigation did not reveal the culprits. Possibly after months in the trenches in a quiet sector the men had been unable to resist the opportunity afforded by a living target. I include the episode merely to demonstrate the great difference between town dwellers and countrymen, who would never have done such a thing.

Rifle Inspection

Provided that rifles are properly cared for, their regular inspection on parade by the platoon officer is little more than a formality. But in my case, the once-in-a-lifetime event occurred, one summer's evening, when I was inspecting rifles before we went up into the line. Rifles are "ported" then in turn moved outward by each individual with the breach open to enable the inspecting officer to look down the barrel to test its cleanliness; then back to "port", the bolt rattled up and down several times, and finally the trigger pressed. On that evening I had come to the fourth man in the ranks and all was normal while I squinted down the barrel and the rifle returned to "port". The bolt was rattled and while I was inspecting the next rifle the trigger was pressed. There was a loud "bang". The rifle had fired and a bullet passed, I suppose, within inches of my face and that of the next man. I can only imagine that the magazine spring was defective and that somehow a cartridge had got jammed in the magazine and was released into the barrel by the action of the bolt immediately before the trigger was pressed. After that for some time I always felt uneasy until rifle inspection was completed without incident.

Exposure

I have always found really cold weather hard to bear ever since my school days when we had cold baths at 6.30 a.m. on frosty February mornings. But those dips were a gentle experience in comparison with the cold in the town of Ypres in the winter of 1917–18. Ypres was still occasionally the target for long distance heavy shells, but these did not worry us nearly as much as the gripping temperatures of many degrees of frost.

Returning from the line we were accustomed to spending a night or two in Ypres before marching further back. I remember standing just outside the remains of the Cloth Hall one winter morning when water was short, saving half an inch of my hot

morning tea for the shaving of my light youthful beard. The operation was somewhat unsuccessful because my fingers were numb with cold. Even colder was the following night when we were dumped in the open beside the bank of a tiny canal with only a ground sheet to sleep on. Never did a night seem to be so long, my whole body perishing with the frost, my fingers too cold even to hold a cup of hot tea in the morning. The endurance of the iron-hard frost still remains in my memory; and Ypres a place of abhorrent exposure.

Kitchener's Army had been slaughtered on the Somme in July 1916 and onwards, and by 1917 the physique of our men was below standard, but they were strong in heart. The first long march of many hours from railhead to the line carrying full equipment was too much for some of them. The stronger of us took over rifles of the weaker brethren. Even then some fell out.

Marching Songs

We did not sing much when marching; other regiments seemed drawn to song rather more than ourselves. Of all the many well known tunes and words of those days I was moved and touched most deeply by the splendour of the tune of *"The Church's One Foundation"* than by other, more popular airs. The tune of the hymn was sometimes sung to ribald words, but its slow rhythm and emotional content enraptured me. On the rare occasions when played in the Anglican church today I picture without fail our lads amidst pouring rain marching through the Menin Gate into a land of mutilation and death. The words of *"The Church's One Foundation"* are of themselves of a quality to cast a spell of hope, for example in the line *"And to one hope she presses with every grace endued"* or again *"And soon the night of weeping shall be the morn of song"*. And in another verse:

> *"Mid toil and tribulation*
> *And tumult of her war,*
> *She waits the consummation*
> *Of peace for evermore"*

That stately, measured tread of sound and vision will be mine and part of me always.

Communication

For substantial journeys we entrained on the slowest most draughty rolling stock I have ever encountered. At one station the train had stopped as usual and I jumped out to make a purchase. Unfortunately for me the train started again and was just leaving the station before I noticed. However I judged correctly and after trotting a quarter of a mile along the line behind it, I caught up and clambered aboard. I was lucky because we were being moved to an important assignment and if I had been left behind through my own carelessness I should have been in real trouble.

I doubt whether there was anything I disliked more than those cold, halting, seemingly endless train journeys to a destination unknown. One was told so little. There seems to have been a lack of communication throughout the War which was unhelpful to us who were to bear the brunt whatever might happen in the line. Personally I should have been happier and less anxious if I had been given some information even in the broadest terms. The degree of dissemination of information had doubtless to be carefully weighed in the balance at any given time, but many of us might have done better had we any idea of the purpose of our manoeuvres. I suppose the security risk had to be considered in case any of us were taken prisoner.

Discipline

As I had never held rank above that of subaltern I had nothing to do with field punishments and the treatment of misdemeanours, and I knew little about them. I suppose that we were fortunate because the possibility of one of my men being court martialled never entered our heads. Their conformity to the essential discipline was taken for granted by me and I am certain that none of them ever had to appear before the Adjutant or Colonel for even a minor misdemeanour. In other companies there were a very few who caused trouble by being slightly insubordinate occasionally or by committing minor offences: they were a nuisance but no more than that, and were presumably dealt with appropriately without great severity.

I trust that no-one who reads these stories and reflections

will think that I was a good soldier. That would be far from the truth as will appear in a short following account of two episodes which illustrate practices of those days, repellant to me then, and today unthinkable. They concern matters to which I could never reconcile myself.

The Court Martial

I was told that I had been appointed a member of a Court Martial to sit on the morrow. I had never attended a Court Martial, let alone sat as a member of the Court. I suppose that during my examinations I may have read something about the subject, but I knew virtually nothing.

Undaunted, I set off in the morning walking across some three miles of open country. At the seat of the Court, a little hut, I met the other two court members, a colonel and a captain from my brigade. I was the junior.

There was to be only one case and without any preliminaries the prisoner, from another brigade, was marched in by a sergeant. He looked a picture, a charming boy of nineteen or so with pink cheeks and blue eyes. I do not remember anyone being present from the Judge Advocate's Department to guide the tribunal on matters of law. Similarly I have no recollection of an accused's friend to conduct his defence and to plead his case. If either were there they said nothing of consequence. In effect the tribunal consisted of us three serving officers with no guidance of any kind and, in my case, with no experience.

The boy was charged with sleeping at his post in the line. This did not surprise me because once or twice on my night rounds I had found a sentry asleep, absolutely worn out, whom I dealt with in my own manner. I myself could sometimes only keep awake by smoking Russian cigarettes, allowing the red hot end to drop into the palms of my hands. I was therefore surprised that a Court Martial was required to adjudicate upon such a charge.

The boy agreed that he had been asleep and as there was no Council for the defence I took the task upon myself of asking him every question that occurred to me from my long experience with a platoon in the front line. How many nights had he been in the line? Had he been unwell? Had he been given enough hot food and drink? What about trench feet, and so on. I really got little response for he made no pretence, simply saying how tired he had been. Nothing was said about his character, length of service, or amenability to discipline. I suppose he was with us about twenty minutes before being marched out. From his temperament and attitude my guess is that he was as ignorant as I was of the seriousness of the charge.

The presiding Colonel then turned to me and said that I, being the junior member of the Court, must speak first. I replied that the prisoner had in effect pleaded guilty and that as a junior officer of the line I would reprimand him. I expressed disappointment that we had no evidence from his platoon commander or platoon sergeant, whom I would consider in a degree responsible. Silence reigned until the Colonel told me that if I found the boy guilty there was only one sentence I could pass. I asked with interest what that was. To my horror he said the death penalty.

I was completely stunned. When I had gathered my wits I spoke to the Colonel and the Captain insubordinately. I pointed out that I lived with my men day and night in the front line, and I understood their utterly overwhelming tiredness on occasion. I described my own methods of dealing with the rare occurrences of sentries sleeping on duty. I would get up onto the fire-step, place my rifle about six inches from the sentry's ear and then fire, shouting at the same moment "they are coming". The effect was dramatic. The sentry would leap into the air, his eyes glazed, startled and staring all around until he saw me on the fire-step. Before he could utter the blasphemy on his lips I said "never again". He learnt his lesson and there was no repetition.

To say the least the Colonel and Captain were unimpressed. Therefore I took a stronger line. I said that I would be prepared to be taken outside and shot, which the enemy would probably do to me anyway before the end of the war, but in no circumstances whatever would I pass the death sentence upon that boy with whom I sympathised. I considered that he ought to have been looked after by his officer and sergeant. Thus the talk continued until eventually I said that if a sentence was essential it must be the least severe. In the end I made the sentence forty days confined to barracks (C.B.), whatever that meant in the line.

Apparently the Court was bound by my decision. The boy

was summoned and told. He showed no emotion, no relief, thus confirming my belief that he had no idea that his life had been at stake. If he had known, his attitude throughout would have been very different. Later in life I have sat as a lawyer in a capital case, when the death penalty was in force, behind the prisoner whose trembling anxiety could not be concealed as the evidence mounted against him.

Afterwards a row really broke out. It started presumably at Army Headquarters and all down the ranks of the very senior officers everybody was blamed for the indiscipline. Eventually the Divisional General sent for the three of us. This indicated the importance the authorites attributed to the case. I told the Divisional Commander that I and I alone was to blame and that he must not be critical of the other two. After my statement the General pointed out that if the death sentence had been passed it would have been reviewed. I did not understand such a procedure, as, to the best of my knowledge, there was no written record of the case. I was not impertinent enough to say so and the General did no more than to express his grave displeasure.

Despite what the Colonel had said at the trial, I never established whether the death sentence was in fact mandatory. If it had been, possibly the proceedings might have been treated as a nullity and a retrial ordered. More likely the regulations provided that a Court Martial sentence, after a verdict of guilty, could not be increased. All was mysterious to me, but I have never forgotten that charming boy with pink cheeks and blue eyes, whose life I have always felt I saved. I can still see his face.

I have told the story to two Field Marshals of the Second World War and to one Commander-in-Chief and all three said that I had done quite rightly. Other senior officers have taken the same view as the Divisional General, that my duty was to obey the regulations and that my independence of outlook was misplaced.

The Execution

Deserters were sentenced to death, rightly so to my mind. The death sentence was lifted only in cases of ill health such as shell shock or mental instability. A man from my company had deserted before I joined the regiment and in accordance with the procedure of the day the sentence had to be carried out by his immediate colleagues of the company. To set an example was possibly necessary in the times of The Duke of Wellington, but it was wholly repugnant to me and an act of cruelty to those who had to carry out the dread deed. In this particular case I doubt whether more than a small proportion of the officers and men of the company had even heard of him or his desertion.

Nevertheless he was sent to us when we were just behind the line. In secrecy one night an officer and a few men were detailed by the battalion adjutant to shoot him on a rifle range the following morning at dawn. The matter was whispered to me and I thanked Heaven that the lot had not fallen to me; I think they feared that I should refuse the order. At breakfast next morning I asked the appointed officer if "it had been done". He replied "Yes", adding however, that he and the squad of men dropped their rifles after firing and fled, running away because they dare not look upon the consequence of their deed. The deserter had been strapped in a chair with a piece of white paper pinned over his heart as a target.

What good could come from such a callous imposition upon the men of my company was beyond my comprehension. I do not recollect the subject ever being mentioned except for the brief words that passed between myself and the officer. I doubt if more than ten per cent of the battalion knew. In any case, in my view, it was an unnecessary deterrent; I myself never saw anything approaching an act of cowardice or even flinching. In my opinion then and now it was an out-dated, outrageous and unnecessary practice. It conformed doubtless to the contemporary regulations, but it was an intolerable obligation forced upon us.

EPISODE SIX

The British

Offensive

Tactics for the Attack

The British offensive was launched on 21st August 1918 and our
division joined the offensive on 22nd August. Our battalion was
known as "the nightjars" because we always attacked during the
night from then on. We never failed to attain every objective we
were set to capture and sometimes we won even more ground.
That is simply a statement of fact, not a boast. Many others
could say the same.

Our Colonel set the attainment of all the objectives on the
shoulders of the leading companies who were ordered to press on
and on, leaving what was called "mopping up" to the following
lines. This was right in my opinion as it would have been im-
mensely difficult to pass a second line through the first on a wet
and dark night in the sequence of a great offensive, which might
be fast or slow – one could never anticipate. So for us of the first
line the motto was "on and on" no matter how many casualties,
no matter how rough the ground or how strong the enemy's
resistance.

We used to attack under what was known as a "creeping
barrage" of shrapnel shells. These burst about twenty feet above
our heads, throwing the shrapnel forward. The barrage lifted at
the rate of about fifty yards every two minutes and our absolute
obligation was to keep ourselves directly under the bursting
shrapnel shells. If one or more of the guns were firing short, that
inevitably meant casualties. The marvel to me was the extraordinary accuracy of the field gunners and those who had made
the fuses of the shells, in being able to provide a barrage line that
crossed the whole of the divisional front, literally to within a few
yards.

Into the Offensive

My platoon was sent in on August 23rd to help recapture a stubborn hill top, which the enemy had retaken, overlooking the village of Miraumont nestling in the valley of the River Ancre. The start of the attack was timed for 3 o'clock a.m. I had a pleasant uninterrupted sleep in a dug-out until called at 2 o'clock to make my platoon ready. We were all so young that sleep presented no difficulty, in spite of the fearful event contemplated a few hours ahead. There were considerable casualties in the attack. The young officer of the other platoon, who had only been with us a day or two, was killed. That was often the fate of newcomers. He hardly got to know his men before being pitchforked into a great battle in the middle of his third night at the front.

For me the advance was comparatively easy but before we were halfway I lost my devoted batman, who had been with me since my earliest days in France. We were side by side when a piece of shell severely injured one of his arms. He screamed to me to stay with him, like so many others in later battles, but of course I had to drive on. I had in effect to push him away. That may sound like rough treatment of an old and trusted servant, always completely faithful to me and to my needs. But split seconds in an attack under a barrage can be of crucial importance especially at a moment such as that when we were passing through the enemy's defensive barrage. Moreover I knew that many lines of reserves were following and that the stretcher bearers would soon find the wounded. Therefore, with sorrow in my heart I carried on with my essential obligation to continue advancing in the attack. Later, when I myself was severely wounded on 20th October, lying only a few yards before an enemy machine gun that was still firing, I personally never felt the need for help and comfort, but perhaps this was because I lapsed into unconsciousness within a minute or two. However it was very common for the wounded to cry out not to be left alone and the rending of one's heart strings in refusing to comfort them tore one deeply, particularly in the case of a long and faithful colleague such as a batman.

The basic rule for the first line in the offensive being to go on and on whatever happened, we never stopped even to search surrendering prisoners. They were the business of others as the attack progressed. When they put their hands up I merely pointed to the rear and signalled to them to proceed there keeping their hands raised. To admit any interference with one's position just under the bursting shrapnel shells was unwise unless inevitable.

Having gained my objective in this attack I was rewarded in the morning with a clear view down into the village of Miraumont. There I could see the enemy moving about, re-assembling after the battle.

By late morning the enemy began to withdraw along the principal road to the East. I passed the word back, and as a result we were given orders in the early afternoon to advance quickly to capture the village. This we did easily, the enemy turning out to be a naval division with little fight left in them. How many prisoners my platoon took I cannot number, although I remember acutely on the main road through the village, as I passed under a railway viaduct in the centre of the village and turned the corner, I walked straight into a German officer. I cannot say which of the two of us was the more surprised. The officer gave no trouble and was certainly looking for an opportunity to surrender.

I was the first person through the village and then on after the enemy retreating up the road. There were casualties and I do not pretend that my men were angels. I strongly suspect that some hand grenades were thrown into cellars amongst cowering Germans.

Intimations of Death

I come now to the great attack of September 27th, to pierce the Hindenburg line. If ever a battle deserved the title of majestic, this was it. At the beginning of that historic night we officers were gathered in a large dug-out for a final discussion. I was sitting next to an officer from another company who began to talk about his past life and the occasions when he had considered he had done ill. I had known others do this and from his first few sentences I knew he was telling me that he would not live the night. In other words he had what I called the mark of death upon him. How one knew is an enigma. There was something about him, his manner, his voice, his words, his spirit utterly different from his ordinary character, all conveying an intangible finality with life here on earth. He was of course killed. Others too, both before and after, revealed to me their prophetic resignation to death. I do not claim any psychic perception on my part, since many others noticed this tendency too.

Anxious Anticipation

Invariably before a large-scale assault we had to be in position in the front line an hour in advance of the action, waiting in a trench, or on the enemy side of a road or river, or lying just in the open. By any standard this was a difficult period because the time passed so slowly. Passing through our minds was an endless procession of ideas about what might or might not happen. How would the battalions fare? What of our company and platoon? Our own fate as individuals? What would be the strength of the opposition? I tried my hardest to find anything to banish the men's dismal fears. I went back and forth continually along the line talking and joking, trying to raise a laugh.

I had rather steady hands and one ploy which I used on tense occasions was to hold out one of my hands palm upwards. Then I went along the line and invited each man to hold out one of his hands just a fraction above mine to see whether either of us was shaking. It caused amusement if one of the men said "Sir, your hand is shaking or quivering more than mine". Childish one might think, but one had to do anything to ease the strain as the minutes ticked so slowly, so dreadfully slowly, away.

On this particular night we were lined up on a sunken track and the moon gave sufficient light for a game. I produced a pocket set of draughts from a haversack and went along the line inviting each man in turn to make a move to win, I myself playing black or white throughout. On other nights I would speak at length about the enemy's defensive position and discuss the tactics at various points of the advance. Literally anything to fend off despondency – the problem was enough to tax the ingenuity of the keenest brain.

A good school master might have managed comfortably. I always felt inadequate.

The Great Offensive on the Hindenburg Line

Our part in the great attack was to be performed as usual at night. We were faced by the tremendous trench systems deemed by the Germans to be impregnable. The night was fine, with a rising moon, and the creeping barrage on a front of three divisions unbelievingly gigantic. The guns were said to be wheel to wheel along the whole front, an exaggeration but it seemed true to us as we moved forward under cover of the barrage with its shattering impact. I wrote a description of this particular barrage in a letter:

"Dawn had not quite broken and a half moon was shining in a cloudless sky. All was as quiet as the grave when suddenly a big gun fired, and instantaneously from one end of the horizon to the other the barrage started. I turned my face behind me and I have never seen any firework display to approach the grandeur. The whole sky from one side of the horizon to the other was lit with flame. The roar of the heavy shells passing right overhead, and the field guns firing shrapnel to provide the creeping barrage was absolutely unbelievable. Seventy yards in front there was a long flickering crashing wall of shells and immediately overhead, no more than twenty feet above us and ten yards apart, the exploding shrapnel shells propelled their lethal contents forward. A barrage is a terrifying thing to be under as always a few men are knocked out by splinters or 'shorts', but it is necessary to keep right under it and prevent the Boche putting his head up before you are on top of him. We would advance and then kneel down for the barrage to creep forward and by the light of the bursting shells I could see right down the line and it was a wonderful sight. The men were in a straight line as though dressed for parade, every man motionless on one knee, the moon glinting on bayonet and steel helmet. As we went forward again the line would break up, the men darting in and out of the trenches and shell holes to clear out the Boche and then back again to the line of the barrage."

I was vastly privileged to have been given a front place at the centre of the mighty clash, a position unequalled from which to see, feel and judge the scene. The gun flashes behind us reached almost to the zenith, the manifestation magnificent. The thunder of the guns, the scream of the shells only feet overhead, their bursting crash, the flicker of rifle and machine gun fire from the enemy lines, the rockets and lights flung up by the defenders were an astounding, all-encompassing experience. The shrapnel bursts of the creeping barrage imparted a compelling urgency of impetus and thrill. Speech was impossible, hand signals being the only method of exercising control.

Aftermath

By dawn we were through the Hindenburg Line. Our objective was reached – an unoccupied valley and beyond it Welsh Ridge was standing in our path. The enemy had been retreating during the night and we were the first to clamber up onto the ridge. We sent a message that delighted everyone concerned but asked for reinforcements against the contingency of the enemy mounting a counter attack. I walked out from the ridge; no enemy was in view beyond the dead and wounded Germans. Then something occurred which has haunted me ever since. I passed a shell hole with a German in it, obviously dying. His lips just framed the word "Vator", but after consideration I passed him by on the other side as the Levite did in the parable of the Good Samaritan. The reason, if one ought to reason when declining to succour the agony of a dying man, being that to drink from our water bottles was absolutely forbidden unless an express order was received. We had no other water and that rule was inviolable. But all my long years I have wondered whether my action could possibly have been right. All that I did in fact was to tell the stretcher bearers where he was lying. I never heard whether he was living or dead when brought in.

The Garden

We came to a stretch of open and undamaged countryside – a marvellous contrast to life in the trenches – and entered and occupied a chateau, which had been an important headquarters of the Germans. The lawns were mown, the borders of flowers still in bloom, lovely in an early autumn evening. But the shock still lingers in my memory. I went out into the garden to post my men. There had been a fight by another regiment before our arrival, of which I had heard nothing; the picture of that fight lay glaring before my eyes when at each turn of the garden's footpaths we came upon the bodies of the young men of that regiment shot down by rifle or machine gun, hardly marked, lying almost as children resting in sleep, in number perhaps a dozen. Why their regiment had not recovered the bodies was never explained to me and we had to do what was necessary.

The poignant contrast on the one hand of the immaculate and peaceful garden and on the other of the sacrifice of such young lives brought tears to my eyes. That graphic and overwhelmingly pitiful picture has often been in my mind as I have walked around the paths and lawns of my own country garden. An episode quite unforgettable and stamped with limitless grief for the evil of the world. That fight must have been the most grisly hide and seek ever played. I once heard a cathedral sermon ending with the words "never forget the garden". The Bible is full of incidents associated with gardens and I speculated whether the preacher, whom I knew well, could possibly imagine what garden was indelibly printed in the mind of this old soldier among his congregation. So lovely, so beautiful, yet so besmirched and desecrated by a deed of war.

A broken, battered Body on the Wire

The climax and end of my military service was at the River Selle. The battalion was immediately south of Solemes, the Germans in a deep railway cutting east of the river Selle a hundred yards or more away. A little bridge had been constructed and we were able to inspect the enemy's position from his side of the river. The fortune of war is entirely unpredictable. This time we had the misfortune to meet the famous Twenty Fifth Prussian Division, which was kept in reserve for emergencies, and claimed never to have been defeated.

As far as our division was concerned the tactics followed the pattern of all our successful assaults, namely a night attack. The front companies were to push right through to the final objective, the higher ground. Once again, I was in the first line. The night was pitch dark with drenching rain. To guide us, the artillery fired a succession of coloured shells pointing the lines between battalions. The conditions were dreadful in the extreme but with a series of successful attacks already tucked comfortably under our belts we were pretty confident; certainly I was, until the moment of truth when we were faced at the lip of the railway cutting by the Prussians. The start was at 2 o'clock in the morning of 20th October 1918, by which time after lying out on the east side of the river in the rain for more than an hour we were drenched and coated with mud.

The barrage, which lifted one hundred yards every three minutes, was greater even than that at the Hindenburg Line. Alas I was left with little more than a glimpse of the awe inspiring spectacle, the dramatic throbbing of the ground, and the totally deafening crash of the showers of shrapnel shells bursting overhead, before I was in the thick of it. I noticed at once a livelier and more comprehensive line of fire from the railway embankment than I had previously encountered. Men were hit within yards of the starting line, the very first being the officer of the platoon next to mine. He went down shot in the neck. Machine guns of the enemy were correctly spreading enfilade fire, one in particular slightly to the right of my advance. I decided that the best course would be for me to walk straight forward to this gun. When just a few yards away I found uncut wire and having fired my rifle from my hip at the gun's flash I put one leg over the wire. Then it happened. I felt that I had been kicked by an elephant. The pain extended over the whole of my lower body and slowly I dropped off the wire. In the words of Studdert Kennedy "a broken battered body on the wire" although not dead.

Before losing consciousness I felt a bullet graze the palm of my hand and a piece of grenade pierce an eyelid. This fragment was eventually found in my forehead. Fifty years later when my back was X-rayed for quite another reason a small handful of grenade shrapnel pieces was discovered in my back. They had penetrated my mackintosh and thick clothing doubtless entering red hot and therefore not creating infection.

Our acting company commander was killed on reaching the railway embankment and the men were left without company officers to lead them before even the first objective had been seriously tackled. The point I want to emphasise is that such loss made not the slightest difference. They all went on under the command of their N.C.O.'s, a discipline firmly understood, and they made the final objective by dawn, after heavy fighting.

Invalided out of the War

I have no idea how long I remained unconscious, but when I came round I was on a stretcher carried by Germans. I assumed that

I had been taken prisoner and shouted to be put down until reassured by an English voice saying that they were prisoners and that the battle had gone well. The fighting in the railway cutting must indeed have been savage. I was told that nearly five hundred German dead were counted there, a not inconsiderable number of men in the context of any ordinary railway cutting I am acquainted with.

I pay the deepest respect to those four Prussian stretcher bearers. They carried me three miles back along the little track which was the only approach to the river at that point. The whole track up to the first field dressing station was still being plastered by the enemy's heavy guns. Yet those dauntless men never wavered one step and bore me as though I was one of their generals. I suppose they knew that they were out of the war, as I knew that I was, and this established I will not say fraternity, but a mutual respect and sympathy not often recorded between friend and foe while still in great danger in the fighting zone.

My preservation seemed unaccountable to me when my mackintosh and map case were decorously returned to me some months later. The map case, which I carried on a short strap just over my heart, had a bullet hole through its centre. I could not count the rents in the mackintosh; it was almost in shreds were bullets and pieces of grenades had torn the cloth away.

The attention at the dressing station was tender and studiously professional. By that time I was not in pain and feeling good once again at the thought of complete victory. I recall a chaplain standing at the foot of my bed pronouncing, to my surprise, what I took to be words for the dying. Then I was taken for an operation which surgeons in London later said had saved my life.

A Final Word

I write at the age of eighty trying not to exaggerate or to over-emphasise. The pictures in the gallery of my mind are as clear and sharp as though they had occurred quite recently. I suppose there were few junior infantry officers serving on the Western Front who survived half the time that I did and then with less than half of my varied experience of attack and defence; many fewer are still living today. I record my remembrances like vivid, bright specks upon a giant canvas partly because by almost any standard they were exceptional in breadth and depth, and captured from the special advantage point of the leading line in attack and the last in retreat.

I have deliberately avoided an historical review of the twenty continuous months that I spent in and out of the line. I leave that to the historians. Instead I have carefully selected, picking out moments to illustrate and maybe to illumine the suffering, the unity of effort, the morale of us very ordinary civilians, and the

dedicated purpose of our actions. We grumbled sometimes, rejoiced at others. All was welded into a way of life that was alien to our natural instincts but demanded by the extended crises of our times. I write from the viewpoint of platoon commander for I was never old enough nor sufficiently developed in character to command a company. Therefore my presentation is from the humblest of commissioned ranks, earth to earth, obeying and conforming rather than conceiving and issuing orders. My post was at the centre of conflict, the perfect place for observation.

Those were happy days of fellowship and camaraderie despite the tragedies. We had no stimulus other than the object of our calling. One of the secrets of our constancy was that there was no emulation amongst us junior officers. Some stayed on with the territorials after the war and gained senior rank, but at the time no one intended to make a career of soldiering. Therefore we were all relatively content with our allotted stations and indifferent to promotion. For the same reason no one was vexed or disappointed when an undramatic role was imposed. It happened that my company was a leading unit in attack probably on account of the outstanding merits of our company commander. But I should never have felt any degree of disaffection if we had been relegated to the second or support line.

This background of no contention for promotion nor vying for distinction had the effect of uniting us in the common effort, encouraging friendship, sharing and mutual respect and, I believe, added much to our simple faithful dedication to whatever task might be directed or ordered. It was a temporary respite of deep and lasting significance, at least for me, from the sharp competitive world that we had left and to which we would return.

I heard that in some companies before a large affair some officers may have had a drink of whisky. But we were always completely stone-cold sober, grasping and adhering to the one purpose – attainment of victory – without attempting to heed or to measure the possible sacrifice of lives and blood. That ideal, if it was an ideal, was part of the ordinary everyday life and never questioned. My little part was a privilege beyond compare. I deem myself fortunate in the extreme to have had such a wide-ranging experience of a war, which now appears to be of special interest to the younger generation who have had no similar experience. I am eternally grateful that so much opportunity was given to me to undertake duties which, looking back, were very risky, yet presented me with a guide for later life, of enduring value and influence upon my career as a professional man. Maybe it is a pity to withhold these simple descriptions from later generations by allowing them to die with me. I have been encouraged to leave these memories to posterity, certainly not for my benefit, but to commemorate the countless number who suffered or died in that titanic struggle.

The Commonwealth War Graves Commission

The Commonwealth War Graves Commission was established by Royal Charter while the First World War was still raging, on 21st May 1917. The Commission has the staggering responsibility of maintaining over one million graves and commemorating a total of 1,694,864 war dead. Of this figure more than one million one hundred thousand originate from the First World War. The magnitude of this assembly defies imagination.

In Belgium and France alone the cemeteries number some three thousand five hundred. In the cemeteries no distinction is made between the great and the lowly; all have the same design of headstone, ranged in line, without regard for military or civilian rank, race or creed.

The Tyne Cot Cemetery contains mostly unidentified bodies and lies adjacent to the very place where I fought in the battle for Passchendaele. The row upon row of headstones are eloquent witnesses of the severity of the fighting in the last stage of the assault upon the Ridge.

The splendid order and beauty of the Commonwealth cemeteries is a tribute to the taste and insight of the Commission. In some burial grounds cottage garden flowers have been planted, a charming touch of simplicity that comforts not only those of my generation who survived but also the host of relatives and descendants of the fallen who visit the cemeteries every year. The idea of introducing cottage garden flowers, with their fragrance and familiarity, to mingle with the dead in their resting place is a perfect touch, entirely appropriate to our Nation. Town or country residents alike, we cherish our little gardens as part of our history and character. Our fallen comrades could not be remembered more graciously or with greater dignity.

In this book I have tried to picture us just as we were, largely simple, naive and homely folk, with one objective only, the fulfilment of the task in hand. During those days of war we young people sorrowed for the loss of our comrades, but looking back I am sure that we did not fully comprehend the blank lifetime grief of bereaved parents. This grief was seldom shown, yet always held within their hearts with unremitting pain. The age of fatherhood gives a sharper refinement. I think of young English maidens, sorrowing and proud, and tearless women seeing pictures in the fire. I think of the days and days that so many of them waited for the telegram, which would finally come to end all hope and to destroy the future to which they had so proudly hung.

Some of the bereaved may have whispered to themselves one of the most sublime and moving passages in the English language, taken from the Scriptures and recounting David sitting between two gates in the walls of Jerusalem awaiting news of his son Absolom. When the messenger arrived and told his story, David went up to the chamber over the gate and wept. And as he went he cried out "O my son Absolom, my son, my son Absolom! Would God I had died for thee, O Absolom my son, my son!".

The Photographs

There was no photographer with Henry Lawson's company in the front line, and the specific incidents described in this book were not, as far as it is known, recorded by photography. These pictures have been chosen to complement the text and to evoke the scenes described, although they may depict different regiments and different points along the front.

Frontispiece Lieutenant Henry Brailsford Lawson, March 1917. *By courtesy of Lady Lawson*

Page 8. Men of the 16th Machine Gun Company, 4th Division, manning waterlogged shell holes on Passchendaele Ridge, 14th November 1917. *Radio Times Hulton Picture Library*

Page 12. Bearing the wounded through Flanders mud. Passchendaele, 16th August 1917. *Radio Times Hulton Picture Library*

Page 15. The Menin Gate Memorial, Ypres, at the great ceremony of Remembrance, 8th August 1928. The Prince of Wales was among 11,000 British Legion War pilgrims at the ceremony. Every evening, to this day, all traffic is stopped and the Last Post sounded at the Gate. *Radio Times Hulton Picture Library*

Page 19. Men of the East Yorkshire Regiment reflected in waterlogged shell holes at Frezenberg, three miles north east of Ypres, 5th September 1917. *Radio Times Hulton Picture Library*

Page 22. Relaxation behind the line. Soldiers fishing in the L'Yser Canal near Boesinghe. Sitting on a duckboard footbridge one fisherman is using a rifle as a rod, the other a barbed wire 'corkscrew'. 28th January 1918. *Imperial War Museum Q10637*

Page 29. British soldiers bathing in the sea at Etaples, 18th June 1917. *Imperial War Museum Q3886*

Page 32. A British sentry alert while his comrades sleep. This trench is at the front line at Ovillers during the battle of the Somme, July 1916. *Imperial War Museum Q3990*

Page 38. Writing home during a lull in the Battle of Messines Ridge at Oostaverne Wood, 11th June 1917. Commanders of some units gave orders that trousers could be cut down to shorts in hot weather, but the High Command are said to have looked down on this form of abbreviated uniform. *Imperial War Museum Q2308*

Page 42. Cheerless surroundings for a feast. These British soldiers are eating their Christmas dinner in a shell hole at Beaumont Hamel, 25th December 1916. Behind them is the grave of a comrade. *Imperial War Museum Q1631*

Page 44. The German Offensive. Two stretcher bearers pause as the German reserves sweep ahead. Each man carries a gas mask in the tin that hangs round his neck. *Imperial War Museum Q55013*

Page 50. The devastation of war. An unidentified road on the Western Front. *Radio Times Hulton Picture Library*

Page 54. An American soldier guarding water supplies during a gas attack. 1918. *Radio Times Hulton Picture Library*

Page 60. A baseball match during a sports meeting of the 3rd Canadian Division at Berthonval Farm, 21st September 1917. *Imperial War Museum C01928*

Page 64. Off-duty artillery officers relaxing outside their billet near St Floris during the Battle of Lys, 2nd May 1918. *Imperial War Museum Q6586*

Page 69. Ypres under snow. A group of soldiers are huddled around a brazier beside the site of the Menin Gate, while empty horse-drawn limbers pass up the Menin Road. *Imperial War Museum Q8356*

Page 76. Under the barrage during the British Offensive. *Radio Times Hulton Picture Library*

Page 83. The Hindenburg Line. This formidable expanse of barbed wire was defended by the Germans with numerous machine gun outposts. This section, at the Beaurevoir Position between Lormissel Farm and Mushroom Quarry, was finally stormed by Australian infantry with tank support on 3rd October 1918. *Imperial War Museum E3583*

Page 88. Passchendaele New Cemetery c.1919. *Photograph by I. L. Bawtree Esq. Imperial War Museum Q100925*

Page 91. The Tyne Cot cemetery at Passchendaele today. *Radio Times Hulton Picture Library*